A Day With

EXCEPTIONAL VISIONARIES

A Day With

EXCEPTIONAL VISIONARIES

MOONSTONE

Published in Moonstone
by Rupa Publications India Pvt. Ltd 2023
7/16, Ansari Road, Daryaganj
New Delhi 110002

Sales centres:
Prayagraj Bengaluru Chennai
Hyderabad Jaipur Kathmandu
Kolkata Mumbai

P-ISBN: 978-93-5702-410-5
E-ISBN: 978-93-5520-942-9

First impression 2023

10 9 8 7 6 5 4 3 2 1

Printed in India

Contents

Walt Disney

Bill Gates

Charlie Chaplin

The Beatles

Walt Disney

Walt Disney was a great animator.
He created many famous cartoon characters.
Read on to learn about his life and work.

Meet Frank and Fiona

Hi, I'm Frank.

Hi, I'm Fiona. We are going to visit Walt Disney. Let's meet him now.

Walt Disney was born in **Chicago**, United States of America on 5 December, 1901. He was a **cartoonist** and an **animator**.

Young Walt Disney enjoyed drawing.
He loved to draw pictures of nature and animals.
He sold his drawings to his neighbours.

Disney also liked photography. He studied art
and **photography** at his high school.

When Walt Disney was 16, the **First World War** was on.
He wanted to join the United States Army.
But he was too young to be a soldier.
So, the Army did not let him in.

But Disney wanted to help. What could he do?
He joined the **Red Cross**. He was sent to France where he
drove an **ambulance**.
He also drew cartoons all over his ambulance.

Walt Disney loved **animation**.
He read many books about animation.
He also learned how other animators worked.

In 1921, he started his own company in **Kansas City** in the United States. He called it Laugh-O-Gram Films.
He made an animated movie called *Little Red Riding Hood*.
He also made a movie called *Alice's Wonderland*.
But he did not complete the movie.

Walt Disney moved to **Hollywood** in **Los Angeles** in the United States. He wanted to be a **film-maker**. But he soon gave up.

He began to make animation movies again. In 1923, he built his first animation studio. His brother became his partner. They called it the Disney Brothers Studio.

DISNEY BROS.

In 1928, Walt Disney created Mickey Mouse.
Mickey's first animated cartoon was named "Plane Crazy".
Mickey also made his screen **debut** in the movie
"Steamboat Willie".
Mickey Mouse became very popular.

In 1934, Disney created Donald Duck.
Donald made his debut in the movie "The Wise Little Hen".
Donald Duck also became very popular.

Chapter 7: Disneyland

Walt Disney loved children.
He wanted to do something special for them.
What could he do?
He built a special park in **California** in the United States.
He called it Disneyland. It was an **amusement park**.
It was the first of its kind in the world.
Now, there are many Disneylands all over the world.

Walt Disney won many prizes for his work.
He also won many Oscars.
The Oscar is a special prize that honours
great work in movies around the world.

Walt Disney was a great animator and entertainer.
He worked hard all his life.
He created many famous cartoon characters that
are very popular today.

Walt Disney died in Burbank, USA on 15
December, 1966.

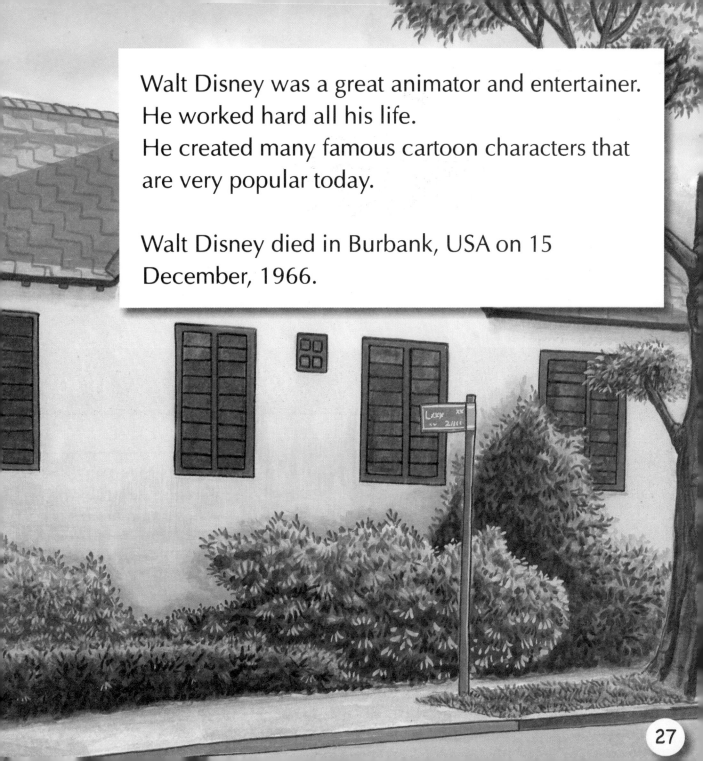

Timeline

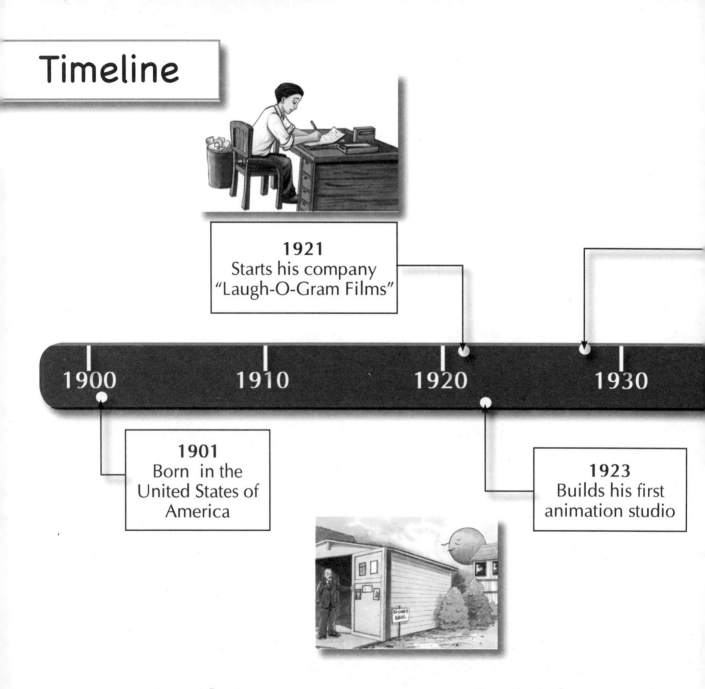

1921
Starts his company
"Laugh-O-Gram Films"

1900   1910   1920   1930

1901
Born in the
United States of
America

1923
Builds his first
animation studio

Walt Disney's Life and Work

1928
Creates Mickey Mouse

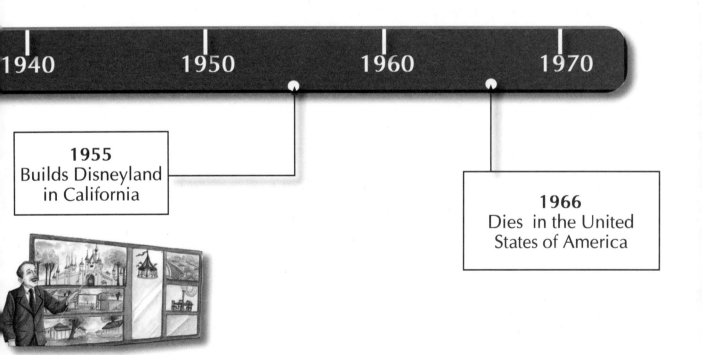

1940   **1950**   **1960**   **1970**

1955
Builds Disneyland
in California

1966
Dies in the United
States of America

Word Meanings

Ambulance: A vehicle that carries sick or wounded people to and from hospitals

Amusement park: A commercial park for entertainment, with rides, shows and food stalls

Animation: A sequence of illustrations shown as a moving picture

Animator: A person who makes animations

California: A state in the western part of the United States

Cartoonist: A person who draws cartoons

Chicago: A city in Illinois in the north-central United States

Debut: The first appearance before the public

Film–maker: A person who makes films

First World War: A war between many nations fought from 1914 to 1918

Hollywood: The home of the American film industry

Kansas City: A city in Missouri in the central United States

Los Angeles: A city in California in the western United States

Photography: The art of creating still pictures

Red Cross: An international group that cares for the sick or wounded during a war

Think, Talk and Write

Think About It

What did you like best about Walt Disney?
Think about why you liked that best.
Draw a picture of what you liked the most.

Talk About It

Tell your family or friends about Disney.
Show them the picture you drew.
Explain what is happening in your picture.

Write About It

Walt Disney wanted to be an animator.
What would you like to be?
Write a few sentences about what would you like to be and why.

What did you learn from Walt Disney?

....

....

....

....

....

....

....

....

....

....

....

....

....

....

What are the five things that you will change after reading Walt Disney's story?

....

....

....

....

....

....

....

....

....

....

....

....

....

....

Bill Gates

Bill Gates is the founder of the Microsoft Corporation.
He is one of the richest people in the world.
Read on to learn about his life and work.

Meet Frank and Fiona

Hi, I'm Frank.

Hi, I'm Fiona. We are going to visit Bill Gates. Let's meet him now.

Chapter 1: In Bill Gates' House

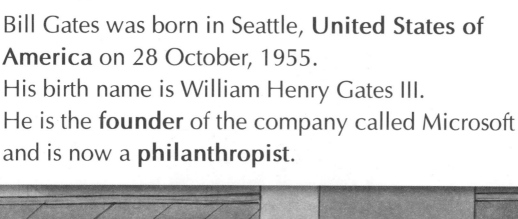

Bill Gates was born in Seattle, **United States of America** on 28 October, 1955.

His birth name is William Henry Gates III.

He is the **founder** of the company called Microsoft and is now a **philanthropist**.

Bill Gates went to a private school.
He was a good student.
He was good at mathematics and science.

At that time, there were only a few computers
around the world because they were large and costly.
Even then, Gates' school bought a computer for all
the students.
Gates was amazed by the computer.
He wanted to learn more about it.
He learned that **programs** ran computers.
He began to write programs.
He read more and more about computers.
He spent most of his time in the computer room
at school.

Bill Gates founded his first company in 1970.
The company was called Traf-O-Data.
His school friend, Paul Allen, became his partner in the company.
They made a small computer.
The computer helped measure traffic flow.
They made a lot of money by selling it.

In 1973, Bill Gates went to **Harvard University**.
But he soon lost interest in studies.
He knew that computers would reach every household in the future.
He also knew that these machines would need software to run them.
So, he wanted to start a **software** company.

The next year, Gates and Paul Allen wrote a computer program.
The program was for a **personal computer**.
It worked perfectly. The software was a great success.
They were ready to start their own software company.

In 1975, Bill Gates and Paul Allen started their own company.
They called it Microsoft Corporation.
It is one of the largest software companies in the world today.

Chapter 6: Microsoft Windows

Microsoft made a new software called Microsoft Windows. It became the most successful software ever. It made Microsoft the richest company in the world. And Bill Gates became one of the richest people in the world.

Bill Gates wrote two books.
His first book was *The Road Ahead*.
It was published in 1995. It was a **bestseller**.

In 1999, he published his second book.
He called it *Business @ the Speed of Thought*.
It has been published in 25 different languages.

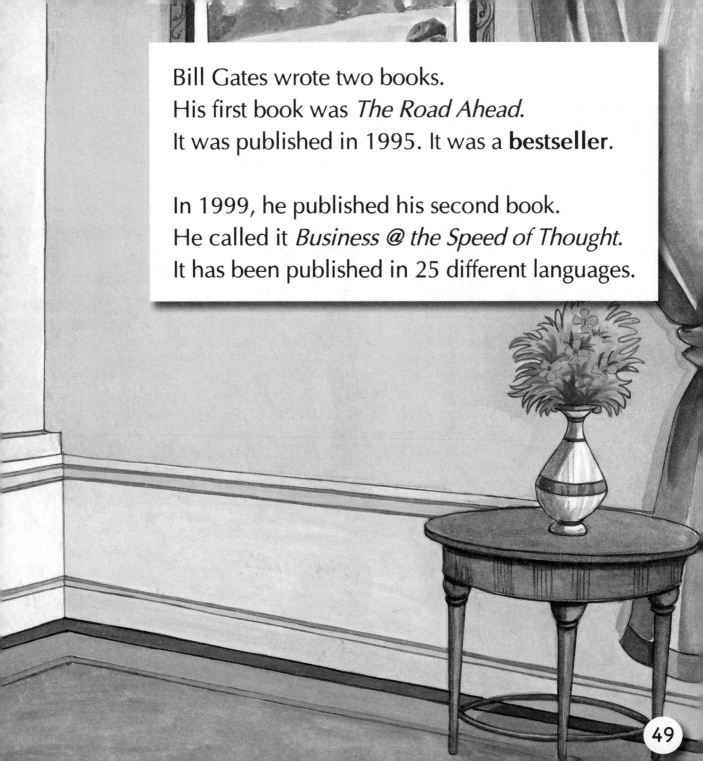

In 2000, Bill Gates and his wife Melinda started a **foundation**.
They called it the Bill and Melinda Gates Foundation.
It is the largest charitable foundation in the world.
It helps people in the United States and other countries.

Bill Gates is an American **entrepreneur**.
He believes in hard work.
He loves reading.
Bill Gates has brought about many changes in the way people use computers at work and at home.

1970
Starts his first company,
Traf-O-Data

1950   1960   1970

1955
Born in the United
States of America

1975
Starts Microsoft
Corporation

Bill Gates' Life and Work

1995
Writes his first book,
The Road Ahead

1980   1990   2000

2000
Starts the Bill and
Melinda Gates
Foundation

Word Meanings

Bestseller: A book that has sold many more copies than others

Entrepreneur: A person who starts a new business

Foundation: An organization that provides money for a special purpose

Founder: A person who starts a new company

Harvard University: A famous university in the United States

Personal Computer: A small computer that you use in your home or school

Philanthropist: A person who does charity

Software: Programs that run a computer

Programs: Instructions written for tasks to be done by the computer

United States of America: A large country in North America

Think, Talk and Write

Think About It

Think about what you just read about Bill Gates.
Bill Gates liked to learn new things.
List two things he liked to study.

Talk About It

Talk with your family and friends about Bill Gates.
Share what you know with your friends or family.
Tell them why you think Gates is important.
Ask them what they know about him.

Write About It

Bill Gates always thinks about doing new things.
What would you like to do?
Write a few sentences to describe your idea.

What did you learn from Bill Gates?

....

....

....

....

....

....

....

....

....

....

....

....

....

....

....

What are the five things that you will change after reading Bill Gates' story?

....
....
....
....
....
....
....
....
....
....
....
....
....
....

Charlie Chaplin

Charlie Chaplin was a great actor and a famous movie star.
He made people laugh through his acting.
Read on to learn about his life and work.

Meet Frank and Fiona

Charlie Chaplin was born in London, **England** on 16 April, 1889.
His birth name was Charles Spencer Chaplin Jr.
He was an actor, writer, **producer**, **director** and **composer**.

Charlie Chaplin was born into a poor family.
He went to school for only two years.

Chaplin's parents were **music hall** entertainers.
He learned singing from his parents.
He loved to perform on stage.
He danced to earn money.

Charlie Chaplin made his stage debut in 1894.
His mother was singing at a theatre when her voice failed
during the performance.
Young Chaplin went on stage and sang "E Dunno Where E Are".
He was only five years old then, and he saved the performance.

Chapter 4: Child Artist

Young Charlie Chaplin joined a dancing group.
The group was called The Eight Lancashire Lads.
The group became very popular.
And Chaplin became famous as a dancer.

Chapter 5: First Film

Charlie Chaplin wanted to act in films.
He moved to the United States of America.
He signed his first film deal with an American film company.
His first film was a silent film called *Making a Living*.
The film was about eight minutes long.
Chaplin played the role of a **trickster** in the film.
It was released on 2 February, 1914.

Chapter 6: The Tramp

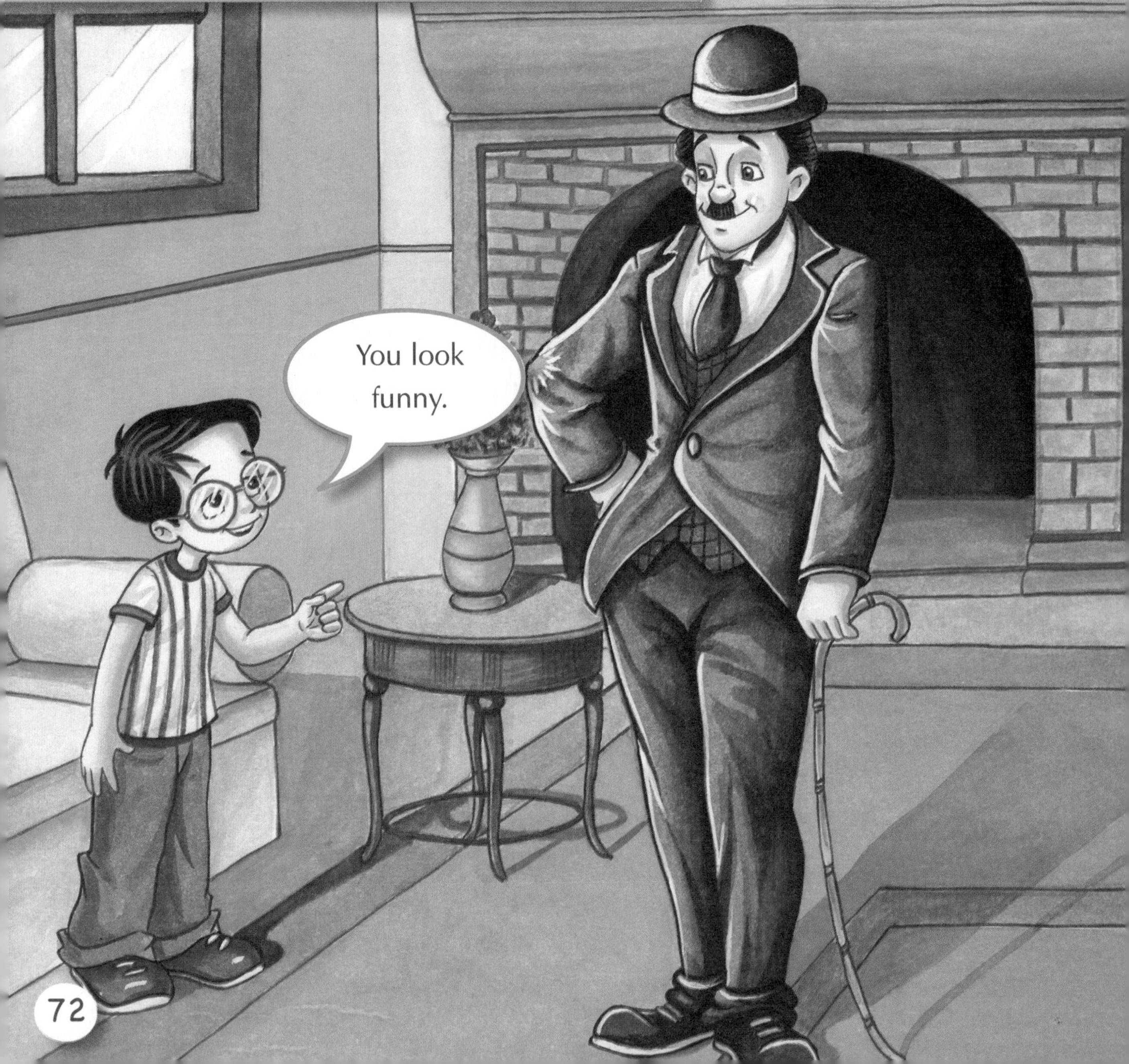

Charlie Chaplin created the character of "The Tramp." His character wore a funny costume. He wore baggy pants and big shoes.

He also used many **props**, like a bowler hat, a bamboo cane and sported a little toothbrush moustache.

The character made him famous and popular all around the world.

Chapter 7: The Director

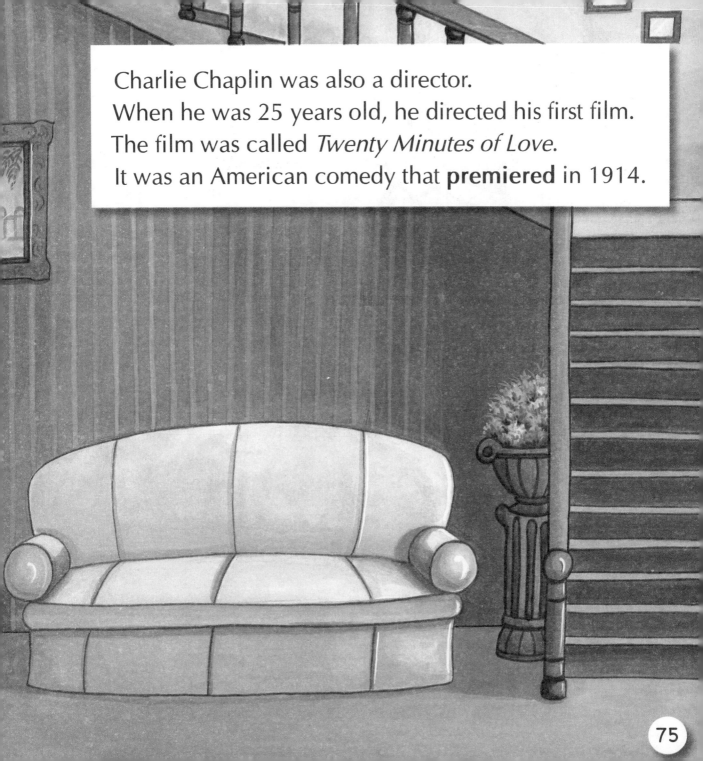

Charlie Chaplin was also a director.
When he was 25 years old, he directed his first film.
The film was called *Twenty Minutes of Love*.
It was an American comedy that **premiered** in 1914.

Chapter 8: Oscar

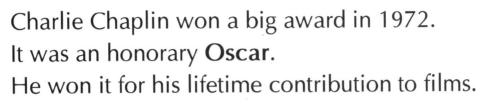

Charlie Chaplin won a big award in 1972.
It was an honorary **Oscar.**
He won it for his lifetime contribution to films.

Charlie Chaplin was one of the most famous film stars of all time.
He made movies into a popular art form.
His humourous character "The Tramp" remains a favourite till date.

Chaplin died in Vaud, Switzerland on 25 December, 1977.

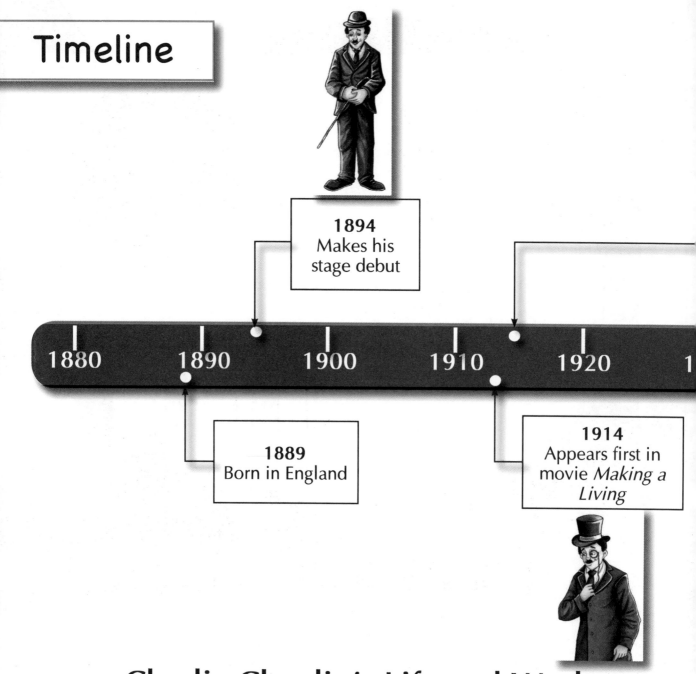

1894
Makes his
stage debut

1880   1890   1900   1910   1920

1889
Born in England

1914
Appears first in
movie *Making a
Living*

Charlie Chaplin's Life and Work

1915
Creates "The Tramp"

1940   1950   1960   1970   1980

1972
Wins an honorary Oscar

1977
Dies in Switzerland

Word Meanings

Composer: A person who creates music

Director: A person who directs the making of a film

England: A part of the United Kingdom, a country in Europe

Music Hall: A form of British stage entertainment. It includes short acts, acrobatics, comedy, and song-and-dance

Oscar: Special prize that honours great work in motion pictures

Premiere: The first official public viewing of a film

Producer: A person who makes movies

Props: Objects used by actors in a scene

Trickster: A cunning character who tricks or cheats people

Think, Talk and Write

Think About It

Charlie Chaplin did many different things.
Which one did you find the most interesting? Why?

Talk About It

How would you describe Charlie Chaplin?
Tell your friends about him.
Talk about what Chaplin did in his life.

Write About It

Charlie Chaplin directed many of his movies.
Think about a movie you would like to make.
What is your movie about?
Make a poster based on your movie idea.

What did you learn from Charlie Chaplin?

....

....

....

....

....

....

....

....

....

....

....

....

....

....

What are the five things that you will change after reading Charlie Chaplin's story?

....

....

....

....

....

....

....

....

....

....

....

....

....

The Beatles

The Beatles were the most famous English rock 'n' roll band in history.

What made them so popular and successful?

Read on to discover the answer.

Meet Frank and Fiona

Hi, I'm Frank.

Hi, I'm Fiona. We are going to travel back in time to visit "The Beatles." Let's meet them now.

The Beatles were the greatest **rock 'n' roll** band of all time. The members of The Beatles were John Lennon, Paul McCartney, George Harrison and Ringo Starr.

All four of them were born in **Liverpool**, England—John Lennon on 9 October, 1940; Ringo Starr on 7 July, 1940; Paul McCartney on 18 June, 1942 and George Harrison on 25 February, 1943.

In 1956, John Lennon started a musical group with his school friends. Lennon was only 16 years old then. They called it The Quarrymen.

Paul McCartney joined the band in 1957 at the age of 15.

George Harrison joined them in 1958.

The Quarrymen broke up in 1959.

In 1960, Lennon, McCartney and Harrison formed a new band. They named it The Beatles.

Ringo Starr joined The Beatles in 1962.

The Beatles began to play in the clubs of Liverpool. At that time, none of the bands in Liverpool played their own music.

They played their own versions of other musicians' records.

The Beatles were the first to write and play their own songs. This made them very popular.

Lennon and McCartney wrote and sang most of the songs.

In 1960, they travelled to **Hamburg**, Germany, where they played at different music clubs. The people of Hamburg enjoyed their music.

The Beatles made rock 'n' roll songs.
They used many new musical instruments in their songs, like **steam organs, orchestras, sitars** and **harmonicas.**

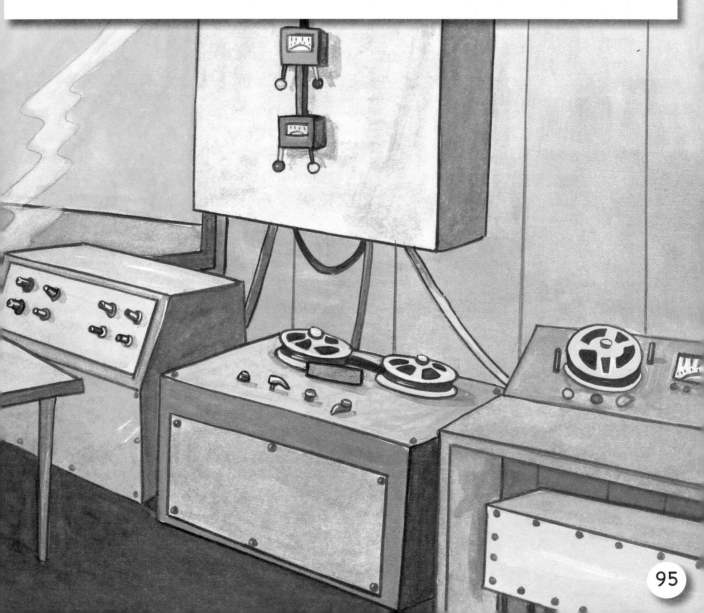

In 1962, The Beatles released their first music record, *Love Me Do*.

People loved their music.

In early 1963, they released their second record. They called it *Please Please Me*.

The record was a big hit.

It became the number one song in the **United Kingdom**.

They went on their first national tour in February 1963.

The Beatles also appeared on British TV for the first time in October that year.

They were seen by six million people across the world.

By the end of 1963, the Beatles had become extremely popular.
Screaming fans followed them everywhere.
Everyone became interested in the Beatles.
Everyone wanted to hear more of their music.
Their popularity came to be known as Beatlemania.

In January 1964, The Beatles released an **album** in the United States of America. The album was called *Meet The Beatles*. It was an instant hit across the country.

In February 1964, The Beatles arrived in **New York City**. The Americans gave them a warm welcome. After two successful shows at the Carnegie Hall in New York, they appeared on a popular television show. The show was watched by 73 million people in the United States. Soon, the Beatles became popular all around the world.

The Beatles appeared in five movies.
Their first movie was called *A Hard Day's Night*.
Their other movies were *Help!*, *Magical Mystery Tour*, *Let It Be* and *Yellow Submarine*, which was an animated movie.

The Beatles were the most popular music band of all time.
They created music that spoke of love, hope, peace and change.
Their songs are still popular all over the world.

The Beatles broke up as a music band in 1970.
On 8 December, 1980, John Lennon was assassinated in New York City, USA. George Harrison died on 29 November, 2001 in Los Angeles, USA.

Timeline

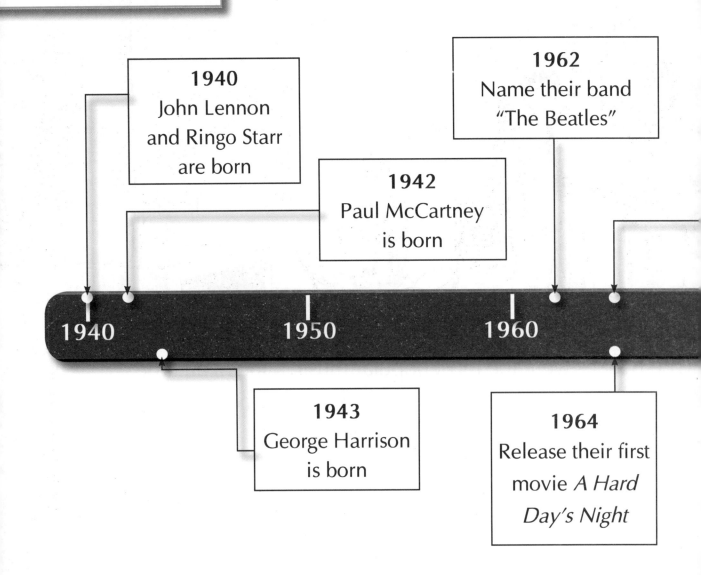

1940
John Lennon and Ringo Starr are born

1942
Paul McCartney is born

1962
Name their band "The Beatles"

1940

1950

1960

1943
George Harrison is born

1964
Release their first movie *A Hard Day's Night*

Life and Work of The Beatles

1964
Perform live in New York City on 11 February

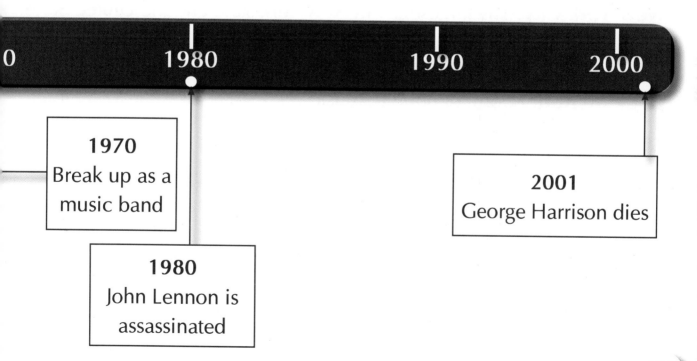

0   1980   1990   2000

1970
Break up as a music band

1980
John Lennon is assassinated

2001
George Harrison dies

Word Meanings

Album: A collection of songs

Assassinated: To murder a famous or important person, especially for political reasons

Hamburg: A port city in northern Germany

Harmonica: A small wind instrument played with the mouth

Liverpool: A large city in northwestern England

New York City: The largest city in New York state and the United States

Orchestra: A large group of musicians playing different instruments

Rock 'n' Roll: A form of popular music

Sitar: A stringed instrument from India

Steam organ: A musical instrument consisting of a series of steam whistles played from a keyboard

United Kingdom: A country of western Europe. It is made up of four parts: England, Scotland, Wales and Northern Ireland

Think, Talk and Write

Think About It

What did you like best about The Beatles?
Think about why you liked them.
Draw a picture of what you liked most.

Talk About It

Share what you know about The Beatles with your friends or family.
Tell them why you think the band became famous.
Ask which one of The Beatles they like best.
Ask what they know about The Beatles.

Write About It

The Beatles wrote their own songs.
They talked about peace and love in their songs.
What would you like to write?
Write a few sentences that describe it.

What did you learn from The Beatles?

What are the five things that you will change after reading The Beatles' story?

....

....

....

....

....

....

....

....

....

....

....

....

....

....

Work Space